I.N.T.I.M.A.C.Y.

Space for Personalized Message

Intimacy: A Poem of Adoration

ACRONYM POETRY GIFT SERIES

By Macarena Luz Bianchi

Illustrated by Zonia Iqbal

 To receive a free ebook, exclusive content, more wonder, wellness, and wisdom, sign up for her *Lighthearted Living* e-newsletter at MacarenaLuzB.com and check out her other poems of self-expression, books, and projects.

ISBN: Hardcover: 978-1-954489-17-2 | Paperback: 978-1-954489-19-6 | Ebook: 978-1-954489-18-9

Spark Social, Inc. Miami, FL, USA, SparkSocialPress.com

Ordering Information: Licensing, custom books, and special discounts are available on quantity purchases. For details, contact the publisher at info@sparksocialpress.com.

All rights reserved. No part of this book may be reproduced in any manner whatsoever without written permission except in the case of brief quotations embodied in critical articles and reviews. For permission requests, contact the publisher noting: Excerpt Permissions.

Copyright © 2021 by MACARENA LUZ BIANCHI

I.N.T.I.M.A.C.Y.

A Poem of Adoration

ACRONYM POETRY GIFT SERIES

Macarena Luz Bianchi

Imprint
Spark Social Press

I love you and our intimacy.

No one else shares this side of me.

Tender and together, we're better.

Intimate and playful lovers.

More and more
connected and adoring.

All of you and all of me,
safe and soaring.

Choosing each other,
every moment of each day.

Your love and our passion thrill me and continue to fill me, with intimacy.

I.N.T.I.M.A.C.Y.
A POEM OF ADORATION

I love you and our intimacy.

No one else shares this side of me.

Tender and together we're better.

Intimate and playful lovers.

More and more connected and adoring.

All of you and all of me, safe and soaring.

Choosing each other, every moment of each day.

Your love and our passion thrill me and continue to fill me, with intimacy.

Thank you, Dear Reader!

Get Inspired & Stay Connected

To receive a free ebook, exclusive content, more wonder, wellness, and wisdom, sign up for her Lighthearted Living e-newsletter at MacarenaLuzB.com and check out her other poems of self-expression, books, and projects. ✨

Your Feedback is Appreciated

If you like this book, please review it to help others discover it. If you have any other feedback, please let us know at info@macarenaluz.com or via the contact page at MacarenaLuzB.com. We would love to hear from you and know which topics you want in the next books. 🌻

About the Author

Macarena Luz Bianchi

Macarena Luz Bianchi has a lighthearted and empowering approach and is affectionally considered a Fairy Godmother by her readers. Beyond her collection of gift books and poems, she writes screenplays, fiction, and non-fiction for adults and children. She loves tea, flowers, and travel.

Subscribe to her *Lighthearted Living* newsletter for a free ebook and exclusive content at MacarenaLuzB.com and follow her on social media. 💝

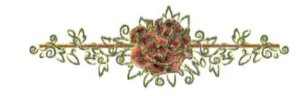

Gift Book Series

ACRONYM POETRY COLLECTION

- *Anniversary: A Poem of Affection*
- *Be My Valentine: A Poem of Love*
- *Congratulations: A Poem of Triumph*
- *Happy Birthday: A Poem of Celebration*
- *Friendship: A Poem of Appreciation*
- *Sympathy: A Poem of Solace*

With more to come including: *Encouragement, Graduation*, and so on.

POETRY COLLECTION

- *Glorious Mom: A Poem of Appreciation*
- *Gratitude Is: A Poem of Empowerment*
- *Gratitude Is: Poem & Coloring Book*
- *The Grateful Giraffes: What is Gratitude?*

Also available for children and in Spanish: Colección de Poesía I.

www.ingramcontent.com/pod-product-compliance
Lightning Source LLC
Chambersburg PA
CBHW061108070526
44579CB00011B/181